Engaging Emotions

The Need for Emotions in the Church

Jamie Dow

PhD candidate, St Andrews University
(Department of Moral Philosophy)
Member of St Paul's and St George's Church, Edinburgh

GROVE BOOKS LIMITED
RIDLEY HALL RD CAMBRIDGE CB3 9HU

Contents

1   Introduction 3

2   How to Misunderstand the Emotions 6

3   The Truth about Emotions 9

4   God Commands Us to Be Emotional 13

5   Why Does God Require Us to Have Certain Emotions? 19

6   Legitimate Emotionalism with no Manipulation 21

    Appendix: 'Firing Up!'—Emotions in Practice 26

    Notes 27

Acknowledgments

I am grateful to Mark Tanner, Mark Melluish, Penny Frank, Jason Curtis, Rich Pratt and Vaughan Roberts for encouraging me in this project, to Mark and Lindsay Tanner, Hazel Dow, Molly Dow, Graham Dow, Penny Frank, Mark Inchley, Cathy Richards, John Taylor, Matt Knowles, Daniel Hill, Alistair Ager and the Grove editors for commenting on various versions of the material and to the Arts and Humanities Research Council for funding the research at King's College London and St Andrews on which this material is based.

The Cover Illustration is by Ian Paul

First Impression October 2005
ISSN 1470-8531
ISBN 1 85174 605 6

Introduction

> The theatre was packed with hundreds, perhaps thousands, of young people. They were on their feet, hands in the air, shouting, 'Jesus! Jesus!' With this number of local young people totally committed to Christ, revival amongst teenagers was surely just around the corner. And yet, this youth leader's heart remained firmly in his boots. For he knew that this was nothing more than music, emotion and adrenaline. The name of Jesus was on everyone's lips, but his impact on their lives was barely skin deep.
>
> The speaker's argument was impeccable. He steadily pressed his case. I knew that it applied to my friends. They needed the forgiveness and reconciliation with God that Jesus brings. It was a miracle of compassion and kindness that God was reaching out to them like this at all! But I also knew that they were totally unmoved by it all. This talk about Jesus was all just arguments and doctrine to them.

We have conflicting instincts about emotions. On the one hand they can be shallow and manipulative. In the wrong hands they are dangerous. Perhaps they bring people to profess faith in Jesus, but such people soon fall away. And yet, on the other hand, something is badly wrong when someone talks about Jesus in an arid and dispassionate way. And who would fault the speaker who moves us deeply at the glory of God, the shame of our sinful lives, the compassion of Jesus or the suffering of a broken world?

So we find a tension in ourselves between approval and disapproval of the attempt to rouse others' emotions

We are deeply suspicious of 'emotionalism'—the deliberate attempt to arouse the emotions of others. Emotionalism has often been the path to manipulation. Yet at other times we find ourselves admiring preachers who are themselves passionate and stir up passion in others. So we find a tension in ourselves between approval and disapproval of the attempt to rouse others' emotions. There is a puzzle here. How can these conflicting intuitions be reconciled with each other?

This puzzle has been the source of some significant tensions between churches. For some, suspicion of emotionalism is stronger; for others, the importance of passion wins out. Furthermore, emotions are sometimes closely associated with charismatic renewal. As a rough generalization, the arousal of emotions in church life occurs more in charismatic than non-charismatic churches. Such emotionalism can thus be a cause of suspicion amongst non-charismatics and a source of lingering unease for charismatics. This is, of course, tangential to debates about supernatural gifts, healing and the like. Nevertheless, a right understanding of emotions will shed light on these suspicions and worries, and will go a long way towards resolving them.

It is crucial for us to relearn the skill of engaging the emotions, deeply and without manipulation

So emotions provide some puzzling conflicts in our intuitions and give rise to some tensions in our churches. However, besides attempting to resolve these, this booklet has a more positive agenda.

It springs out of a conviction that it is crucial for us to relearn the skill of engaging the emotions, deeply and without manipulation. We are suspicious of emotions because we do not understand them. However, once we discard common misunderstandings and come to a more accurate view of what the emotions are, their importance for the church becomes obvious.

This passion for emotional wholeheartedness is not entirely new. It is, however, largely forgotten. Jonathan Edwards, the American puritan preacher, philosopher and theologian, wrote a *Treatise Concerning Religious Affections* in 1746. He affirms unstintingly the importance of the emotions in Christian discipleship and in church life.

> We may hence learn how great their error is, who are for discarding all religious affections, as having nothing solid or substantial in them.
>
> There seems to be too much of a disposition this way, prevailing in this land at this time. Because many who, in the late extraordinary season, appeared to have great religious affections, did not manifest a right temper of mind, and run into many errors…hence religious affections in general are grown out of credit with great numbers, as though true religion did not at all consist in them. Thus we easily and naturally run from one extreme to another.[1]

One of the ironies of Edwards' legacy is that many of the churches today that most revere him are among the most averse to emotion!

Like Edwards, I write as a philosopher and theologian. The case for understanding and responsibly engaging emotions is made therefore partly from everyday experience and common sense reflection, but it comes most clearly from God's word. It should be most compelling to those who have a love for the Scriptures. My argument here is that if we disregard the emotions we disregard a central call of God upon our lives.

If we disregard the emotions we disregard a central call of God upon our lives

I argue that emotions are not to be thought of as mysterious sub-rational forces sweeping through us from somewhere deep within. Rather, they are cognitive and part of our rational minds, responsive to circumstances and hence motivators of (rationally justifiable) action. My hope is that we can relearn a wholehearted discipleship, in which the emotions are fully engaged. Clearly we must not endorse every use of emotion uncritically. We will need a good framework of understanding to help us distinguish between legitimate emotion-arousal and shallow manipulation. Working within such a framework, we will be in a safe position to seek wholehearted passion throughout our church life.

Questions for Reflection

1 How do you view emotions at present?

2 What strategy or understanding do you currently have of the role of emotions in your own (and your church's) spiritual life?

2 How to Misunderstand the Emotions

People's views of the role emotions should play in church life tend to depend on what they understand emotions to be.

Those who are wary about the stirring of emotion in evangelism, preaching and worship tend to justify this by an implicit appeal to a certain view of what the emotions are. Likewise the case here for a more positive attitude towards using emotions rests crucially upon an answer to the same question, 'What *are* the emotions?'

The Traditional 'Irrationalist' View of Emotions

The traditional view of emotions characterizes them with words such as 'irrational,' 'fleeting' or 'unpredictable'; it associates them with 'personal baggage.' Seen from this perspective the emotions lie at the opposite end of a spectrum from rational argument, careful thought, logic, science, truth, careful investigation and reason. They are sometimes associated with our lower, animal, bodily nature as part of a contrast with the mind and our higher, thinking, nature.[2]

Most adherents of this view are disparaging of the emotions. Emotions are irrational, and lack the reasoning control of the mind. They are unpredictable and often fleeting. Hence we have good reason to be wary of them and avoid giving them any pivotal role in church life. However, some who are very positive about the emotions also see them according to this traditional irrationalist view. The emotions may not be reasonable, logical or rational—so much the worse then for reason, logic and rationality! Such an approach can be characteristic of those who see logic and argument as nothing more than vehicles of domination—of women by men, the uneducated by the establishment educated, and so on. On this view, logic, argument and rationality are to be thrown aside in favour of the intuitive, the emotional, the artistic, the feminine. But both the positive and the negative view share a similar irrationalist conception of what the emotions are. As we shall see, this represents a gross misunderstanding of the emotions.

This erroneous view has been hugely influential, not just historically within certain schools of psychology, but also within the church. It is used by some churches to justify a non-emotional, rather traditional, carefully controlled style in public worship. For other churches, this view of the emotions leads to an embarrassment about the arousing of emotion as part of worship or preaching. Vaughan Roberts writes about the effect of congregational church music as follows.

> A friend of mine refers to 'the liver shiver.' I guess we know what he means. No doubt there have been moments when we have felt our whole bodies tingling. Our emotions have been switched on, and it has been almost as if we have been transported out of ourselves.[3]

The phrase 'liver shiver' encapsulates beautifully the traditional irrationalist view of emotions.[4] They are bodily phenomena, fleeting experiences with something rather mysterious about how and when they occur. No wonder Roberts concludes that they cannot be good indicators of God's presence.[5]

It will become clear that this is an inadequate view of the emotions. Moreover, it has served to impoverish our church life because of the unease about emotionalism that it has engendered. So how has this view gained such popularity?

Culture and Psychology

We may suggest two reasons for this misunderstanding. Firstly, in Britain there is a cultural reticence to be emotional and this is reflected in our churches. It may be that this reticence is compounded by factors related to who holds power within the church—a predominantly male church leadership is perhaps one.[6] It has been comfortable for us to believe that emotions are irrational and untrustworthy, and that it is acceptable to keep our church life pretty dispassionate.

It has been comfortable for us to believe that emotions are irrational and untrustworthy

Secondly, our understanding of the emotions has been predominantly shaped by pastoral psychology. The traditional irrationalist view has some evidential basis, and this is crucial in understanding how to pastor and counsel those seeking help when things have gone wrong. Even in everyday cases, we know how flawed emotions can sometimes be. Emotions sometimes involve distortion, overreaction, getting things wrong or out of proportion and clouded judgment. They can impede personal growth, destroy relationships needlessly, and make it hard to relate to God. They can be influenced by bodily factors—lack of sleep, hormonal changes, hunger, alcohol, and so on. If one's view is formed mainly from this kind of evidence, the evidence of *problematic* emotions, it is easy to see the attraction of the irrationalist view. Historically, this view has been influential within some branches of psychology, and its influence on pastoral theology is still considerable.[7]

One reason for the continuing popularity of this view among some working in pastoral counselling is that it immediately delivers an accepting approach towards the emotions of a client. If emotions are non-rational, bodily phenomena, then they are as morally neutral as a tingling or nausea or an itch—not right or wrong or justified or unreasonable. It is obvious that this accepting, neutral stance is useful in a counselling situation. Furthermore, some emotional patterns are not easy to change. This too might seem to suggest that it makes no sense to evaluate emotions as right or wrong or reasonable.

The effects, however, of this irrationalist understanding have been considerable. The emotions have been confined to a marginal role in church life. It may be good to express emotions in sung worship and perhaps emotions can be allowed a place in good relationships between Christians. Preachers might occasionally be encouraged to think about how to engage the feelings of congregations, although this is usually accompanied by a note of caution. To the irrationalist, the mind should first be persuaded, and only then (if at all) the emotions aroused, once the truth has been apprehended.[8] But these are all concessions—in the church the emotions are mostly best ignored.

Within some churches, this serves as a justification for dry, academic teaching, a carefully controlled worship culture, and a wordy intellectualism that is more rooted in an academic culture than in scriptural obedience.[9] Even in more lively churches, where emotions are engaged in preaching and worship, there can often be a significant contingent who find such an approach hard to justify. There is a fear that emotions are sub-rational forces being used to manipulate people. Thus, for some, the irrationalist view serves to prop up culturally-driven prejudices about worship and preaching style. In others, it hinders clear thinking about the boundary between healthy engagement of emotions and unscrupulous manipulation.

My main objection to this irrationalist view, however, is that it is false—it fails to give an accurate picture of what the emotions are. The inadequacies of the irrationalist picture become clearer on comparison with a more cognitive model.

Question for Reflection

Do you recognize elements of this 'irrationalist view' in your or your church's approach to the emotions?

The Truth about Emotions   3

Emotions are ways in which we grasp how things are in the world.

That is to say that they are rather like beliefs, convictions, insights, knowledge, or perceptions—ways of grasping for the truth.

> Imagine someone says to you, 'I'm very angry with Mike.' When you ask her to explain, you find out that she thinks that Mike is kind, generous and thoughtful. After asking her questions for a while, it seems that there is nothing she thinks Mike has done wrong. You would surely be puzzled— how can she be angry with Mike if she thinks he's done nothing wrong?

The puzzle over this scenario highlights a very important feature about the rationality of the emotions. In order to make sense of her anger at Mike, we needed to understand some wrong that she thinks Mike has done. This is because anger *involves thinking that someone has done some wrong,* normally against oneself. Likewise, fear involves thinking that something bad is threatened. Pitying someone involves thinking that that person is suffering undeservedly, and so on.

Emotions typically involve three interrelated components.

1 *A belief-like component* In any emotion, we take things to be a certain way, we 'feel that' things are that way. The object of the emotion is held to have certain features. When we love someone, we think that they are valuable, or (more accurately) we 'feel that' they are valuable. When we are jealous of someone, we are feeling that they have something that we should have; when we feel sad, we feel that things are bad; when we feel excitement, this involves feeling that something good is going to happen.[10]

2 *A motivation component* Emotions typically motivate us to action in certain ways. Pity motivates us to help; anger to strike out; jealousy to take back what should be ours; fear to avoid danger; and so on. Not every emotion has immediate motivational effects, but most are connected directly or indirectly with the motivation.

3   *A distinctive 'feel' or 'phenomenology'* Emotion episodes are accompanied by bodily changes: a rush of adrenaline; feeling hot or tense; knots in the stomach; the heart beating faster. The way in which the distinctive phenomenology of emotions is related to the other two components is somewhat contested. My preferred view is that two things are happening. First, the beliefs/motivations involved in the emotion themselves have a distinctive feel. Second, the emotion causes various bodily changes, such as sweating or tensing of muscles, which also have a distinctive feel.[11] In the past some psychologists thought that emotions essentially consisted in their phenomenology alone, and that this was the way to study emotional experience.[12] It is now clear that the phenomenology of emotions is rather coarsegrained. The bodily states and phenomenology of different emotions are not hugely different from one another, and assessments of a person's level of arousal are too crude a measure to tell us much of interest about emotional experience.[13] If we only consider the 'feel' of emotions, it becomes very difficult to distinguish them from each other. Embarrassment often feels very similar to anger.

These components have been described as they relate to emotional episodes. These are central to emotional experience. But we should also note that in speaking of 'emotions,' we often refer to enduring states. 'Mary has been angry with her mother for twenty-five years,' does not normally mean that she has been hot with anger continuously over that period. It means she has had a continuing tendency to feel angry from time to time over that period. Enduring state emotions are dispositions or tendencies to have episodes of felt emotion. We often speak, rightly, of loving someone as an enduring state in which the feelings that are essential to it may be felt only occasionally.

The belief-like component of emotions has some important features. For each kind of emotion—anger, pity, compassion, love—the emotion has what I shall call *'proper objects.'* For example, the proper object of love is something valuable. (When you love someone, you feel that they are valuable.) The proper object of fear is something threatening. Now, in every case of emotion, we feel that the object of our emotion is a *proper* object of that emotion. When you are afraid of a spider, you feel that it threatens you some harm. This is of course not to say that our emotions always *correctly* latch onto their proper objects; the spider may not actually be able to harm me, sometimes I am happy at something that will really turn out to be very bad, and so on. The claim here is that emotions, like beliefs, involve thinking that things are a certain way. Like our beliefs our emotions are fallible, they do not always get things right.

It follows that emotions may be justified or unjustified, warranted or unwarranted. They are justified when they latch onto their proper objects. This is a perfectly familiar feature of emotions which is obscured by the irrationalist picture. If there is nothing threatening harm, then my fear is unjustified. If there is no possibility of Scotland winning the World Cup, my hope is misplaced! Likewise, one's emotion may be out of proportion to the circumstances. If someone pushes ahead of me in the bus queue, I might justifiably bear them some resentment. But if it is still burning inside me a week later, it is out of proportion to the original wrong. If someone holds a door open for me, I should perhaps feel grateful, but I should not feel indebted to them for life!

Thus far I have argued from simple common-sense observations of everyday life, supported by some empirical research. Yet the picture emerging is just what we find reflected in the Scriptures. Later chapters will engage more fully with the scriptural material. For now, let us note how the Bible corroborates the picture given. Cain and Jonah are both challenged as to whether their anger is justified (Gen 4.6; Jonah 4.9)—they are angry, but have they really been wronged? Jesus feels compassion for the crowd who are harassed and helpless (Matt 9.36). Likewise, he advises the disciples about fear—it should be directed not at those who threaten comparatively little harm, but at fear's proper object, the one who has the power to inflict the greatest harm of all. 'Do not fear those who kill the body but cannot kill the soul; rather fear him who can destroy both soul and body in hell' (Matt 10.28). Emotions have proper objects, and are justified when directed at these, unjustified when not.

This understanding is a long way from the irrationalist picture. Imagine the conversation of the Emmaus walkers in Luke 24, from the irrationalist view. 'Were not our livers shivering within us while he was talking to us on the road?' It is ludicrous! In reality their hearts were burning with emotion, with excitement, and this was no merely-bodily, irrational, meaningless phenomenon. It was typical emotion, a rationally sensitive emotion, responding with excitement to the truth that here in Jesus all God's Old Testament promises were fulfilled. If ever emotions were rightly directed to their proper objects it was here.

The motivation component is equally significant. Its vital importance is in moving us towards action. In both everyday life and in the Bible, we find acts of pity (Luke 10.37) and compassion (Luke 7.13), crimes of passion, usually involving anger and jealousy (Gen 4.1–8; Prov 6.34). Fear makes us avoid the object of our fear (Gen 3.8). Anger is a motivation to punish (Dan 3.19). Even where there is not such a direct connection with motivation, as with shame, pride, disappointment or admiration, the belief-like component will always be evaluative, and so will influence our motivation accordingly. A shameful action is one we have some reason to avoid in future. Similarly, feeling that my achievements are marvellous is likely to motivate me to talk about them. Disappointment typically leads to adjustment of expectations or avoidance of risk.

A further observation about emotions should be made. They are not under our *immediate* voluntary control, but they are to a significant extent under our *long-term* voluntary control. We cannot feel pity just by exerting our will. No amount of careful concentration and gritting of the teeth will produce an episode of excitement. But we can over time harden ourselves to the suffering of others, or learn to respond compassionately. Anger can be brought under control. Things that once brought fear can become familiar and hold no fear for us, and so on. We can learn to love people who initially seemed to us utterly unlovely. Perhaps there are limits to this control, and the reality may be that the Holy Spirit stands behind all such emotional change. The power of prayer in these areas is well-known. Nevertheless, the generalization holds good— our emotions are to a significant extent under our long-term voluntary control.

From this brief sketch of what the emotions are, a number of important conclusions follow.

1   Emotions are ways in which we grasp the truth and are motivated towards action.
2   Consequently, they are central to discipleship. They should be of critical interest to anybody interested in discipleship.

Pastors, teachers, church leaders, catechists and mentors are all seeking to help people apprehend the truth about God and be motivated to live accordingly.

3   It is therefore astonishing that the emotions are so neglected in the mainstream activities of church life.

This is the central claim of this booklet. The emotions should be central in church life. If we have a right understanding of our emotions we will be well placed to engage them constructively for the kingdom of God.

God requires of his children that they respond to him not just with right action, but with right emotions—our godliness should go deep within us. The Scriptures have a great deal to say about this, so now we turn to examine this biblical material in more detail.

Questions for Reflection

1   Can you identify within yourself these three elements of an emotion?
2   How good are you at responding positively with right emotion?
3   What skills do you need to develop to train the emotions within yourself or your church?

God Commands Us to Be Emotional

4

It is not often recognized that a significant part of what the Lord requires of us as Christians is to have the right emotional responses.

We tend to think that our Christian obedience consists of actions, behaviour, how we speak, where we direct our thoughts, our use of money, time, and the like. We might think that developing virtue or godly character is important, insofar as godly character involves dispositions to act and think and behave rightly. It is less frequently recognized that godly discipleship also involves having the right emotions. Still less is it realized how substantial a part of discipleship this is, and how prominently it features in the Scriptures.

Now, this seems puzzling—emotional episodes are, in significant measure, involuntary. How can God require us to do something that is not within our voluntary control? Under the influence of this (partially correct) line of thinking, apparent biblical instances of God commanding us to have certain kinds of emotion have been subjected to 'behaviourist reinterpretation' as commands to *act* or *behave* in certain ways. So when we read such lines as 'get rid of…anger, wrath, malice' and, 'clothe yourselves with compassion, kindness, humility, meekness and patience,' (Col 3.8, 12) what we hear is a command simply to exhibit certain patterns of *behaviour*, rather than a command to have right *emotions*. And yet anger, wrath, malice, compassion, kindness, humility, meekness and patience are all inner emotional states. Our pervasive tendency to behaviourist reinterpretation of Scripture blinds us to the prevalence of emotion language in the Bible.

I will make the case against behaviourist reinterpretation in more detail below. First, however, let me establish the centrality of right emotions in the Christian life. The case for their placement at the centre of our discipleship is so vast and pervasive that I can only illustrate it here. I will consider Jesus' summary of the law, look at the very nature of God and then briefly consider some of the emotions commanded in the New Testament. In chapter 5 I will then consider why God wants us to engage with the emotions he has given us before finally addressing the question of whether a behaviouralist reinterpretation is valid or necessary.

The Greatest Commandments

> 'Teacher, which commandment in the law is the greatest?' [Jesus] said to him, 'You shall love the Lord your God with all your heart, and with all your soul, and with all your mind. This is the greatest and first commandment. And a second is like it: "You shall love your neighbour as yourself." On these two commandments hang all the law and the prophets.' (Matt 22.36–40)

Jesus is asked to rank the commandments of the law and pick out the greatest, the most important. He picks out two commandments, both of which are commandments to love. So ingrained is the tendency to behaviourist reinterpretation that we scarcely notice that, on the face of things, these are commandments to have emotions of a certain kind.[14] We are commanded to have the emotion of love towards God and towards our neighbour. Not only that, but Jesus suggests that the whole of God's requirements are summarized in these requirements to have right emotions of love towards God and neighbour. Jesus is saying that if our emotional life is fundamentally well-ordered at the centre, then this will result in all of the other aspects of obedience that God requires. Let us not miss the significance. *Jesus puts emotion at the centre of discipleship*. On his authority, we are to understand that the entire Old Testament has this emotion at the centre of discipleship. And just the same view is endorsed by Paul at Romans 13.8–10. Love, an emotion, directed at its proper objects—God and neighbour—is central to the whole of what God commands us. (Do notice how absurd it would be to think of this merely as a 'liver shiver.' Emotions of love are central to discipleship because they involve both a *recognition* of the immense value of God and neighbour and a *motivation* to act accordingly in sacrificial service.)

Jesus makes this selfless emotion a distinguishing feature of the community of his followers

The commandment to love one another is prominent in Jesus' upper-room discourse, and he makes this selfless emotion a distinguishing feature of the community of his followers (John 13.34–5; 15.12–17). When Peter is restored after the resurrection, before he is given any practical commission, Jesus' first and foremost concern is to establish whether or not Peter loves him (John 21). According to Jesus, love for God, love for him, love for neighbour, love for fellow-believers are central to being his disciple. In short, Jesus summarizes the life to which he calls us in emotional terms.

The Character of God

> The LORD passed before him, and proclaimed,
> 'The LORD, the LORD,
> a God merciful and gracious,
> slow to anger, and abounding in steadfast love and faithfulness.'
> (Exodus 34.6)

This formula, echoed many times through the Old Testament, is fundamentally a revelation of God's nature. It is intended to convey what God is like. It speaks of God's emotions, his feelings.[15] He is characterized by mercy, kindness, plenty of love and loyalty, and a certain sluggishness when it comes to anger.

What we see here can be stated very simply. The most central and important features of God's character in the Scriptures are described in emotional terms.

A list of these attributes makes the point crystal clear. God is a God of love. He is a God of pity and great compassion. He is slow to anger, but his anger or wrath is aroused by disobedience and wrongdoing. He is a jealous God, upset when the love and adoration that should be his are directed upon some other object. He is a God of great sorrow over the brokenness of his world. These attributes are not peripheral to the revelation of God's nature in the Scriptures. It is these emotional characteristics that are central to any explanation of God's dealings with humanity. In particular, it is God's anger, love and pity that explain Jesus' death for us.

We see these aspects of God's nature reflected in Jesus himself. He is one who weeps with compassion (Matt 9.36; Mark 7.11–15; John 11.35). He is angry at hardness of heart, at dishonour to God, at harshness to children, and perhaps angry at 'sin, sickness and death' itself (John 11.33;[16] Mark 3.5; 10.14; 11.15–17). He is, of course, above all the man of love who gave up his life for his friends (John 15.13).

The emotional character of the Holy Spirit is less prominent. Nevertheless, the Holy Spirit can be grieved (Eph 4.30) so, at the very least, the Bible gives us this glimpse into the Spirit's emotions.

It is frequently acknowledged by Christian writers, even amongst those deeply in the grip of the irrationalist view, that emotions are natural and inevitable and part of our God-given nature. We can now see that merely making this concession is far too cautious. Emotions are central to the nature of God himself. They are not just a natural and inevitable part of our human make up, but part of the image of God in us. In right and godly emotions, we most wonderfully reflect the glory of God himself.

Furthermore, if Christian ethics may be understood as seeking to be like our heavenly Father (as suggested at Lev 11.44-5 and Matt 5.48), right emotions must be central to obedient righteousness for us too. Indeed, when we look at New Testament ethics, this is precisely what we find.

The New Testament Gives Emotions a Central Place in the Christian Life

Love

It will already be clear that if love is recognized for what it is, a cognitive, rational, mental and motivational emotion, then here is one emotion that is foundational to obedient Christian discipleship. We have seen this in Jesus' teaching. For the apostle John too, love is not only the mark of a Christian—the means of knowing that we have passed from death to life (1 John 3.14)—but loving in the right way encapsulates the whole of the Christian life. To live obediently is to love one another and to cease to love the world (1 John 2.15; 3.11). We find similar sentiments in James, Peter and Paul (James 2.8; 1 Peter 1.22; Rom 13.8–10). Indeed, throughout the New Testament, what is sought is a love that reacts with genuine feeling to others, because of their value as people, and to God because of his immense worthiness.

Excitement

Next, consider excitement. The proper object of excitement is something wonderful that is either about to happen or is already at hand. We have already seen the excitement of the disciples on the road to Emmaus at Jesus' fulfilment of Old Testament promises (Luke 24.32). Likewise, for us, excitement should characterize our Christian lives, as we discover more about Jesus and more about God's purposes (2 Cor 4.6, 16–18). As we grow to Christian maturity, we should never lose the sense of thrill at hearing the voice of the Lord and learning more from him, just like those Emmaus walkers.

Joy

At Philippians 4.4, we are emphatically commanded to rejoice! Rejoicing is having the emotion of joy, and we are repeatedly commanded to direct it towards its proper objects, such as the Lord, his salvation, his resurrection, the gospel and the growth in the Christian life of others and ourselves (Phil 4.4; 1 Peter 1.8; Matt 28.8; 1 Thess 1.6; 3 John 4; James 1.2). Our ability to be obedient to this command springs not from a direct ability to turn emotions on and off at will—we do not have such an ability. Rather we have control over various associated activities. So we can control what we let our minds dwell upon. We are able to allow ourselves to experience joy without being embarrassed about it. This is how we can develop a capacity for joy that is directed at its proper objects, at genuine grounds for rejoicing.

Sorrow and Regret

Sorrow and regret have a core role in the life of discipleship as the appropriate emotions to accompany repentance (2 Cor 7.8–11; Acts 2.37; Luke 6.21, 22.62, 23.28; James 4.9). Paul commends the Corinthians for their godly grief that led to repentance, and he contrasts godly sorrow with worldly sorrow. Godly sorrow is a felt response to things that are bad, involving a motivation to change for the better. So, this is a paradigm of an emotion containing the three components of belief, motivation and 'distinctive feel.'

This godly grief is to be contrasted with a worldly counterpart which we might better call despair. Despair may often be out of proportion to its object. It may fail to take proper account of the sovereignty and mercy of God, and hence falsely represents things as beyond redemption. It contains no motivation to change.

Gratitude

A further example, gratitude, will make it clear how central emotions are to the Christian life. There is scarcely a book of the New Testament that does not contain an injunction to be thankful. In particular, Colossians 3.15–17 hammers out the command three times in three verses! After all that God has done for us in Jesus, it is simply obvious that our hearts should be characterized by gratitude.

Admiration, awe, fear, pride, tender-heartedness, and others could be traced through the New Testament in a similar way. Some might wonder how pride, jealousy, anger or fear could have an appropriate part in the Christian life but there is no real difficulty. My contention is that these emotions also have their proper objects. So, just as with other emotions Christian disciples should have feelings appropriate to each situation, likewise with these emotions. Sometimes this will mean no emotion at all, a state of serenity or calmness.[17] Likewise, some emotions should be scarce in the Christian life, because we are rarely faced with their proper objects. Three examples illustrate the point.

Anger

The Scriptures are cautious when it comes to anger for a number of reasons (Eccles 7.9; Prov 16.32; Matt 5.22; Gal 5.20; Eph 4.26, 31; Col 3.8; James 1.19–20). We are often mistaken about when wrong has been done. We frequently set too high a regard on our own projects, plans, desires and dignity. So when these are harmed we are more prone to anger than we should be. Jesus' own example is deeply challenging (Phil 2.3–8). It suggests that *most of the time*, we have too little humility and too high a regard for ourselves. As a result, our anger is frequently unjustified and wrong. Indeed the Lord himself is 'slow to anger'—meaning he restrains himself from anger, even where it would be justified, in the hope that repentance and obedience will occur.

Fear

In the case of fear, there is scarcely any scriptural command more repeatedly given than the command not to be afraid (for example Gen 15.1; Josh 1.9; Isa 41.14; Dan 10.19; Luke 12.32; Rev 1.17). This does not mean that all fear is inappropriate. We have seen that Jesus gives specific instructions on whom to fear (Matt 10.28)—we are to fear God and not other people (see also Deut 6.13; Josh 24.14; Ps 33.8; Ps 34.9; Prov 3.7; Rom 11.20; Heb 4.1; 1 Peter 2.17). The reason why God's people are so repeatedly told not to be afraid is because we have a great tendency to unwarranted fear. When we lose sight of God's power and goodness, then threats of harm will seem of greater significance than they really are. We so easily forget God's sovereign power, his care for us and his astonishing ability to bring good out of the darkest situation.

Jealousy

Jealousy might seem to be an emotion with no place in the Christian life but again this is not the case. After all, it is part of God's character (Exodus 20.5). It should be part of ours, rightly felt if the circumstances are appropriate.[18] Jealousy has a proper object, like all emotions. It is a feeling that someone else has something that should be mine, and involves a desire to have that thing restored. So, God rightly feels jealousy when his people give to something else the adoration and allegiance that should be his. Likewise, you would be right to feel jealous if your spouse's intimate affections were directed towards someone else. Such jealousy would ideally never be actualized. It is this disposition that the Lord has in relation to his people. Envy is misdirected jealousy, and as such is always sinful; it involves wrongly thinking that something should be mine, along with the desire to possess it.

Questions for Reflection

1 How does this understanding of the emotions affect the way you will teach the Scriptures?

2 Try turning to a Psalm and reading it aloud with this chapter fresh in your mind. How can you begin to train your emotions biblically?

Why Does God Require Us to Have Certain Emotions? 5

Emotions, we have seen, are both truth-directed and motivational. They are ways in which we grasp for the truth, that spur us to action.

A pattern of emotional response is a pattern of motivation. Where this happens correctly it is the driving force in virtuous character.[19] These facts alone explain why our emotional lives are important to God. He wants us to apprehend the truth and live consistently in the light of it. Right emotions help us to do this.

Furthermore, right motivation and action is much more effectively achieved with the cooperation of the passions than without them. Dispassionate dutiful obedience is hard to maintain and can be less than wholehearted.[20] Emotions, however, tend to be deeply embedded and produce long-lasting effects on our behaviour. Once trained they are difficult to deceive. Whilst our conscious thinking can be misled by clever arguments, our emotional patterns tend to be much slower to change.

Emotional patterns also tend to 'infect widely' within our psychological make-up. That is, emotions have a rapid, automatic, and powerful influence on many aspects of our thinking, motivation and behaviour, in ways that go far beyond the inferences that we are able to make consciously. Imagine a child discovering to her shame how she has hurt someone through thoughtless insensitivity. The effect of this emotion serves to make her more sensitive to others, keen to avoid repetition of the wrongs of the past. Perhaps she could work out by conscious reasoning how her behaviour ought to change. But her emotions will normally do a much more efficient and comprehensive job here than she could ever do by conscious reasoning. Of course, we can sometimes react emotionally to our experiences in ways that hinder our future lives. But in general, we are created in such a way that our emotions regulate our future thinking, feeling and behaviour in ways that are highly effective and beneficial.

So the Bible's emphasis on Christian character is intimately tied up with our emotional lives as well as with right action. Living a life of humility, gentleness, patience and love, being kind to one another, tender hearted and forgiving (Eph 4)—these virtues involve consistent patterns not just of behaviour, but of motivation and feelings. In short, the importance of Christian character and virtue brings with it the importance of right emotions.

Behaviourist Reinterpretation of Emotion Language

The above sketch has shown how there is no need to reinterpret, in purely behavioural terms, God's commandments to love and to have other right emotions. They do not need reinterpretation. They make sense as they stand.

When the disciples are urged, 'Love one another' (John 13.34), they are being commanded to have an emotion. But we should notice also that this is a command with implications. Love is an emotion that includes a motivation to seek the good of the person loved. The command is not fully obeyed if the motivation is unaffected. Consequently, to obey this command is already to be set on the path to action. The obedient disciple will feel a certain way, and will be motivated to serve others in a way that is directed towards putting this into practice. This very point is made by both Jesus and the apostle John (John 13.21–4; 1 John 3.14–18).

One reason for the popularity of behaviourist reinterpretation is the fact that scriptural commands to have right emotions often have specific practical implications. The observation of these implications is correct, but it is an inadequate reason for the behaviourist move. We are very familiar with this use of language. We say to a child, 'Be a good boy,' in a situation where what we intend is that the child should stop pulling his sister's hair. Commanding the child (literally) to have a virtuous character has obvious immediate *implications* for behaviour. Likewise, 'Put away all malice' is literally a command to end wrong emotions, but it has the immediate *implication* of requiring an end to all malicious actions. Behaviourist reinterpretation is not required in order to bring out these implications. To reinterpret the Bible text in a way that dismisses the everyday sense of the emotion words is something that risks disrespecting the text and diluting the demands of discipleship. Such reinterpretation would be legitimate only if there were good reasons for it and such reasons are clearly lacking. The Bible has both emotional and dispassionate language, and we should not obliterate the distinction between the two.

Right emotions, then, are central to and crucial for godly discipleship. They may not be under immediate voluntary control, but this does not mean we have no control over our emotional lives. On the contrary, there is a great deal we can do to develop the emotions that God demands. It is for this reason that we must engage the emotions as part of corporate church life.

Questions for Reflection

1   Do you recognize the Lord's call on your emotional life?
2   How do you need to respond to this in your own discipleship and that of your church?

Legitimate Emotionalism with No Manipulation

6

The Case for Engagement of Emotions in Church

Right emotions are a significant part of obedient discipleship; they are prominent in what God requires of us, and they are a vital means to purity, holiness and godliness in thought and action. Growing obedient disciples is a central part of the church's mission. Our church life should therefore help us towards having right emotions. It will fail to do this if it leaves the emotions untouched in preaching, worship, prayer and evangelism—indeed in any area of church life.

We urgently need to learn the skill and sensitivity required to engage the whole person, including the emotions, in ways appropriate to cultures and personalities. This applies as much to the engagement of non-Christians in evangelism as to Christians within the church.

Further, if we do not engage emotions, we risk communicating falsehoods. A dispassionate presentation of God's judgment implies that it is not important enough to warrant fear or urgency. Telling the stories of Jesus without seeking to warm hearts and kindle a love for him will seem to imply that there is nothing here worthy of such feelings. Dispassionate talk about our tendency to materialist desires suggests that these are nothing to be ashamed of. Likewise, worship of Jesus for his death for us should be suffused with gratitude, or else it risks belittling the benefits he has lavished upon us by his death. In short, dispassion risks telling lies about the Lord.

However, we clearly need boundaries. We need to know how to arouse the emotions legitimately without manipulating people. Not just any engagement of emotions will do—manipulation dishonours the image of God in people, by failing to respect their full humanity. So, we need to understand what is appropriate and acceptable in engaging the emotions.

Legitimate Engagement of Emotions

Here is a kind of checklist for legitimacy. Where these guidelines are violated, there is a risk of manipulation. Where they are observed we can have confidence that people are being treated properly as we encourage fully-engaged, wholehearted discipleship.

The Emotions We Try To Arouse Should Be Justified

We have seen that emotions have proper objects. A justified emotion is one that is directed at and proportional to its proper object. Another way of saying this is that the object should *merit* the emotion. Jesus' death for us merits the gratitude of the whole of our hearts and lives—it is hard to imagine how one could be too grateful for all he has done for us. Nevertheless, the emotion should be a response *to* that proper object, and not simply triggered by music or art. So, there seems something illegitimate about encouraging people to commit their lives to Jesus in gratitude to him if they have been presented no good grounds for that gratitude. It is very tempting, especially in youth work where clarity of communication is so important, to simplify the message of an event so much that one calls for an emotional response, without giving good grounds for that emotion. It would be manipulative to urge gratitude to Jesus without presenting the cross or some other good grounds for gratitude. Emotions should be justified by being directed at their proper objects.

Emotions Should Be Engaged in the Apprehension of Good Reasons

As we have seen, emotions are a way of grasping the truth in a way that motivates us to act in the light of that truth. Consequently we need to be careful about what motivations we stir up. When people are emotionally aroused, they can be easily manipulated to respond in certain ways. We want emotions that motivate action in a way that is supported by good reasons.

If the Holy Spirit has given you the gift of tongues, this is a good reason to give thanks humbly and to use the gift for the building up of the church or for speaking privately to God. It is not a good reason to look down on other members of the church (1 Cor 12.4–11, 21; 14.1–5).

Arrogant words dishonour God and this is a good reason to change the way I talk. It is not hard to see that shame, regret and sorrow would be a powerful way in which to recognize this. On the other hand, such shameful arrogance is not any good reason for self-harm, although one can see how someone might think so. The emotions of shame, regret and sorrow are only appropriate when they arise from good reasons and are focussed towards humility and change.

Thus we can see that emotions must be aroused in apprehension of *good* reasons. Those who serve or lead the church (in any capacity) need carefully to consider the opportunities this presents to engage people's emotions in a godly way.

There is actually a huge opportunity here. Consider an evangelistic presentation of the gospel. Within a simple gospel outline, there are many opportunities to engage people's emotions:

- God's astonishing power and artistry in creation warrant admiration, awe, wonder, delight and thrill at all that is good in the world.

- God created us, owns us, and we owe our whole lives to him—it is appropriate to feel a strong tie of obligation to him.

- There are good grounds for shame and guilt in how we have treated God, his world and other people.

- Yet, despite all of this, God has dealt with us in Jesus with kindness and mercy far beyond what we deserve—a sure ground for immense gratitude to him.

- In fact when we consider what God has done for us in Jesus, the welcome into his family, and the hope that lies ahead for us, a full appreciation of this is likely to leave us overwhelmed with emotion.

We see here a number of legitimate opportunities for engaging the emotions in a way that runs deep, encouraging a right response to the gospel of Jesus Christ.

We Must Not Bypass Dispassionate Thought, But Rather We Must Help It Keep Up and Enable People to Give Enduring Assent

Manipulation often uses emotion to override the control of calmer thinking and the will. That is, it looks for an emotional response that would not be given at a more dispassionate time. For instance, it is dangerous just to use images that are hard to follow, even if the emotions stirred are subconsciously justified and in line with good reasons. Put simply, we want people to be able to assent to the responses, commitments and convictions they form, in a way that makes these of enduring and lasting value. We need to engage the whole person in a way that respects and honours each person's richness and complexity, including dispassionate as well as emotional rationality and responses. To do this requires us to ensure that dispassionate thinking keeps pace with the emotions. So, in preaching, points should be clear, easy to follow and memorable, as well as emotionally compelling. In prayer ministry people need to be enabled to respond emotionally to their loving Lord and take steps of faith which may previously have been inhibited, but the minister needs great skill and sensitivity to help them understand what is happening and not to push someone further than they choose to go.

This guideline is not best met by running away from all emotion. Neither should dispassionate thinking be dominant and emotional thinking optional and secondary. We have seen that this over-cautious approach risks telling lies about Jesus and about the gospel. Such an approach foregoes great emotional resources for building disciples. Rather, we should aim ideally to engage *both* emotional *and* dispassionate thinking. Both can at times take the dominant or primary role, but neither should be neglected. Both represent important parts of the personality whose force should be enlisted in helping people to believe the truth and live lives worthy of the Lord.

Keep Open a Sensitivity to a Full Range of Relevant Considerations
One of the real strengths of our emotions is that they give us a drive and focus that can be vital at critical moments. Nevertheless, this feature of emotions brings risks with it. If a particular emotion is engaged, it is easy to become blind to other relevant considerations. When we are seeking an emotional response in others, we need to ensure that we are not blinding them to relevant considerations to which they need to maintain a sensitivity. Thus encouraging young people from non-Christian families to give Jesus their 100% allegiance, will involve encouraging a sense of admiration and gratitude towards him. But it is not right to do this in a way that blinds them to their need to honour their parents.

One aspect of moral maturity is wisdom (James 1.5). Wisdom involves a kind of '360-degrees' sensitivity to considerations pertinent to a situation, and the ability to weigh these correctly. It is important that when we engage emotions, we do not do so to the detriment of wisdom.

There is a particularly high risk of narrowing our sensitivity when fear is aroused. Fear is a powerful emotion. It makes us highly responsive to the object of fear yet simultaneously can render us blind to other considerations. It is for this reason that politicians frequently use fear to persuade and manipulate. Sadly, fear is sometimes used this way even within the church. For example, some use fear of heresy in order to control the kind of Christian books others read. It is not uncommon in some university ministry for there to be an unspoken canon of which authors and publishers are 'sound' and which are not. A very cautious and heavily controlling approach can inadvertently become prevalent. Now, it is legitimate to fear the effects of error. Nevertheless, for this fear to prevent oneself learning from other Christians because their books are not 'approved,' for this fear to lead to an unhealthy dependency on a circle of the influential few, for this fear to discourage wrestling personally with Scripture and with contemporary issues with all the fire, creativity, vigour and thirst for truth that can be mustered, is for fear to have become manipulative.

An excellent example of getting this whole dynamic right was seen recently in the youth work of a large Christian conference in Scotland. During the course of the week, the emotional temperature varied considerably. During the main talks, speakers spoke carefully and persuasively from the Bible. At times there was no holding back their passion in speaking of Jesus, his death, and the life of discipleship. With great skill, speakers engaged the emotions of the teenagers in seeing how God's call applied to them and in feeling an urgency to respond. Nevertheless, at moments where the young people were asked for decisions, conclusions and choices, the emotional temperature was kept cool. Such decisions would have life-changing implications for their faith, relationships and very lives. There was a deliberate strategy of ensuring that the young people had space and the right atmosphere to consider properly how they might respond. This was partly a matter of enabling their dispassionate thinking to keep up with their emotions. However, it was also in order to engage emotions in a way that kept open a sensitivity to other relevant considerations.

This is how things were handled at times of decision. Then, during times of praise and thanksgiving to God, there seemed no restraint to the engagement and expression of emotion. Song lyrics put God's glory, his love and Jesus' sacrifice at the centre of attention, and gratitude and adoration poured forth. Why the contrast? Participation in emotional times of worship was principally based upon existing convictions. These were not times to *persuade* people of God's love or of Jesus' sacrifice. Rather, they were times for believers to express commitments they already had. Of course, as this happened, God worked to deepen these commitments, and lives were changed. Furthermore, there was no expectation that complex life-decisions would be worked through during these times. On this basis, times of praise and thanksgiving could be made a 'safe' environment in which to arouse strong emotions, even with a kind of abandon, a total focus on God. This skill and sensitivity to provide at different times for both careful deliberation of complex decisions and for exuberant celebration of God's goodness, and to vary the emotional temperature accordingly, is something that is a highly estimable quality in a church leader.

These guidelines provide a basis for emotional engagement that is responsible and legitimate. Armed with this understanding, we can steer clear of manipulation, and still confidently engage the emotions throughout church life. The emotions are so crucial in Christian discipleship that it is vitally important that church leaders learn to engage people relevantly and deeply and personally. As our emotions are engaged, they can be a powerful and lasting way for our love and obedience to grow. I end with something of my own story…

…fifty teenagers sat looking at me, as I sobbed my way through the story of the prodigal son. Desperately trying to control my voice, I told them of God's immense love for them. What had happened to me? Ten years ago this would have been unthinkable! Yet now, when leading worship or teaching the gospel, I frequently well up with tears.

I have gradually learned to engage my emotions in praise and prayer. My teaching and leading have also become more emotional. God has used Christian musicians and artists to help me here, but especially preachers and leaders. Each time I have taken a step forward, I have been challenged to take yet another! In the end I have become convinced that emotions convey important truths, and are part of building up wholehearted disciples. I thank God for those leaders who have stirred godly emotions in me. I pray we may learn the same skill for the sake of many others.

Questions for Reflection

1   In what ways do you already seek to engage emotions in your ministry?
2   Have you been guilty of manipulation? How might you avoid this in future?
3   In what aspects of your ministry do you need greater engagement of emotions?

Appendix:
'Firing Up!'—Emotions in Practice

Here are some exercises to help you consider how emotions can have a rightful place in your personal life and church life.

Preaching

- Review some recent talks. What kind of response was being sought— to what extent did they aim at stimulating appropriate emotion?
- Introductions / Illustrations / Ending. How can you use each section to engage emotional responses that contribute to the purpose of the talk?
- Aiming for the very best. How can you adapt your preaching style and skill so that it aims not just at conviction and understanding alone, but also at passionate engagement of the heart?
- Assess the level of emotional vulnerability of your audience. How should this affect the way you engage their emotions?

Evangelism

- In what ways do you use the arousal of emotions in evangelism?
- How can you use the emotions to enable non-believers to feel the full force of the truth of the gospel, and yet still allow them space and freedom in relation to their response?

- For an evangelistic talk, think about the particular emotions you wish to arouse. How can you give the listener really good grounds for each emotion? How can you direct these emotions properly towards trust in Jesus?

Worship and Music
- To what extent are worshippers given a good basis on which to feel godly emotions, directed properly at the Lord and all he has done for us? Is the information content of our songs too heavy, too light or about right?
- What styles can you use to help people to engage emotionally with prayers or Bible passages?
- What can be done musically to give the congregation the best possible help in engaging emotionally with God? Think about speed, introductions, explanation of words, links between songs, the sequence of songs and musical style.

Training for Christian Ministry
- Compare the value given to dispassionate argument compared to well-directed emotional response within training for ministry. How well does this fit with biblical discipleship?
- When in their training are church leaders helped to develop skill and insight in engaging the emotions of those they teach and lead?

Personal Life
- Look back over chapter 4. To what extent are the patterns of your own emotions in line with what pleases God?
- How often do you allow your emotions to be fully engaged by God's truth?
- If your personal or church situation makes it hard for you to be emotionally engaged by God's truth, where can you find contexts in which to grow and express your God-given emotions?

Notes

1   Jonathan Edwards, *Treatise Concerning the Religious Affections* (1746), part I.
2   M Nussbaum, *Upheavals of Thought* (Cambridge: Cambridge University Press, 2001) pp 24–6; A Kenny, *Action, Emotion and Will* (London: Routledge, 1963); T Dixon, *From Passions to Emotions: The Creation of a Secular Psychological Category* (Cambridge: Cambridge University Press, 2003).
3   V Roberts, *True Worship* (Carlisle: Authentic Lifestyle, 2002) p 87. This view surfaces within arguments directed (rightly) against a claim that musical praise causes us literally to enter

God's presence and against the view that an emotional experience enables us to know infallibly that we have encountered God.

4   Roberts, *True Worship*, p 28, 'True worship will certainly involve our emotions, but it does not begin with them. Worship is rational; it involves the mind.' Also John Stott, *I Believe in Preaching* (London: Hodder, 1982) p 282, 'the combination of mind and heart, the rational and the emotional.' Note how the emotions are contrasted with 'mind' and 'rational' in both writers.

5   Roberts, *True Worship*, p 88.

6   Other possible factors may be more controversial, such as the disproportionate influence of public school or Oxbridge education, or the predominantly academic character of leadership training in the church.

7   By contrast, Cognitive Behavioural Therapy (CBT)—prominent today in clinical psychology—involves the kind of cognitive view of the emotions recommended here.

8   J I Packer, *Evangelism and the Sovereignty of God* (Downers Grove: IVP, 1961) pp 82–91, whose thinly veiled attack on the Billy Graham crusades gives absolute primacy to 'the mind' (which, in his view, excludes the emotions). Virtually silent on engaging the emotions are John Stott, *I Believe in Preaching* (London: Hodder & Stoughton, 1982), and Richard Bewes, *Speaking in Public Effectively* (Fearn: Christian Focus, 2002).

9   Roberts makes the same point, *True Worship*, p 96.

10 Note that emotions may have a vague object. We feel anxious that 'something bad,' we know not what, is going to happen. In this respect, ongoing emotional moods such as depression are no exception, as is sometimes thought. In depression, 'things generally' are represented as hopeless.

11 A Damasio, *Descartes' Error—Emotion, Reason and the Human Brain* (New York: Grosset/Putnam, 1994), part II.

12 C Lange and W James, *The Emotions* (Baltimore: Williams and Wilkins, 1922).

13 S Schachter and J E Singer, 'Cognitive, Social and Physiological Determinants of Emotional State' *Psychological Review* 69 (1962) pp 379–99.

14 Some argue that love is not an emotion, but is about choice and actions, for example M Scott Peck, *The Road Less Travelled* (London: Rider, 1978) part II. This seems mistaken and offers no advantage over the view of love as an enduring state emotion, or tendency to emotion.

15 This does not necessitate a denial of the doctrine of divine impassibility. At most, this doctrine should be construed as entailing the denial that God has emotions imposed on him from outside. In contrast with the irrationalist view, the cognitive view of emotions presented here involves no threat to impassibility thus construed. The view of divine impassibility such that God has no emotions at all is rejected by Wayne Grudem, *Systematic Theology* (Leicester: IVP, 1994); John Piper, *The Pleasures of God* (Fearn: Christian Focus, 2001) and Richard Swinburne, *The Christian God* (Oxford: OUP, 1994).

16 D A Carson, *The Gospel According to John* (Leicester: IVP, 1991) pp 414–6.

17 Some psychologists think we are always in *some* emotional state. They might insist on redescribing a state of no emotion as one of low physiological arousal.

18 Num 25.10–11, on which Mark R Talbot 'Godly Emotions (Religious Affections)' in John Piper and Justin Taylor (eds), *A God Entranced Vision of All Things: The Legacy of Jonathan Edwards* (Crossway, 1994) ch 10, available online at http://www.gnpcb.org/product/1581345631.

19 Aristotle, Nicomachean Ethics II.6.1106b24–27 and II–VI generally; Aquinas, Summa Theologica IaIIae.59; S Hauerwas, The Peaceable Kingdom (Indiana: Notre Dame, 1983) chs 1–3.

20 2 Cor 9.7 'God loves a cheerful giver.'